Safety Inside the Circle

Save Sex for Marriage - but Why?

Written and illustrated by Christine Lauren

To order additional copies, search by title and author's name at www.amazon.com or put www.createspace.com/3498143 in URL, not the search bar.

Contact author at feetadancing@gmail.com

ISBN Number: 145633218X
EAN-13: 9781456332181
Printed in the United States of America

Bible quotations are from The Holy Bible, New King James Version, Copyright 1982, Thomas Nelson, Inc., The Holy Bible, King James Version, The Rainbow Study Bible, Copyright 1981, and the New International Version, The Student Bible, The Zondervan Corporation, Copyright 1986.

Cover Art and book layout by Kina Forney: www.kina-ink.com
Copyright 2005

Foreward

I dedicate this book to young adults around the world. You are our future. I also dedicate this book to all the parents, grandparents, pastors, teachers, youth ministers and countless others who dearly love our younger generation and have been crying out for a voice to address the issue of sex outside of marriage and its consequences.

I believe this book answers that cry. There is only one solution to this dilemma, or any human dilemma; that solution is the truth found in the Bible, the living and powerful Word of God.

For that reason, this book is based on the Bible. Everything else will fade and pass away but the Word of God endures forever.

My prayer is that your life will be enriched and blessed as you read and digest the contents of this book. And beyond enrichment and blessing, may it bring you freedom and joy in your life.

With love,

Christine Lauren

Acknowledgements

A note of thanks and appreciation to Elizabeth Kandrac,
Charles Hughes and Phil and Roxy Rust
for their editorial help.

A special note of thanks to Kina Forney for her rendering
of the drawings on pages 23, 34 and the drawing for the
"Heartbreak Prevention Quiz."

In addition, a special thanks for the use of the
"Bare Tree by Fence" drawing used on page 40 at
www.wpclipart.com.

TABLE OF CONTENTS

PART ONE: FOUNDATION

1. Introduction

I want you to be happy!

As you read this book and apply what it says, you will find your life changing in wonderful ways. It will guide you into:

- Friendships that last

- True closeness and security

- Respect for yourself and others

- Mental and emotional health

- Powerful self-esteem and a sense of well-being

- Knowledge of your true identity

- Purpose for your being on planet earth

Let's get started!

2. But Why Not?

Be a winner! Say "no" to sex...but why?
What principles could possibly produce such dramatic effects in your life to fulfill the list you just read? What power is behind the truth of these principles?

Let's find out!

Why is it right to save sex for marriage? You may be thinking, but why not have sex? Everybody's doing it!

No, everybody's not doing it! Please read this article from "Dear Abby," a newspaper columnist who gives advice on a variety of topics.

Readers praise Abby for 'no' advice to 17-year-old virgin

DEAR ABBY: Three cheers and blessings upon you for telling "Hurting in Hartford" -that 17-year-old virgin- that she is neither weird nor stupid for sticking with her principles. She'll never lose a guy who's worth having if he drops her because she refused to have sex with him. In fact, she's lucky to be rid of the creep.

I was a 24-year-old virgin when I got married, and I've been happily married for 26 years. I never had any guilt, illegitimate children or venereal diseases. If more girls stayed virgins until they got married, we'd have a healthier world, a lot less misery and lower taxes. SUZIE IN MOBILE, ALABAMA

DEAR ABBY: I'm glad you told "Hurting in Hartford" to hang on to her virginity. If I'd been as strong as she seems to be, I wouldn't have lost mine at 15. It has taken me 8 years and four relationships to learn that a relationship built on sex doesn't last.

If the fear of pregnancy doesn't keep her out of the sack, the fear of AIDS should. That, and the desire for a permanent relationship, is what have kept me from making sex the payoff for a date. I learned the hard way that if a guy really cares for you, he won't ask you to do anything you're not ready for. Giving in at 15 was the dumbest thing I ever did. LEARNED TOO LATE IN ROCKFORD

DEAR ABBY: This is for "Hurting in Hartford" whose relationships never lasted any longer than three weeks because she wouldn't have sex with her dates. Please, keep on saying NO. Putting out will not win you popularity. It will only get you a bad reputation because no matter what a guy says, he will talk about you afterwards to other guys.

I didn't put out and I was popular. Sure, there were guys who tried to score with me, but when they knew they couldn't, they respected me and remained my friends anyway. Deep down in my heart I knew I was saving myself for someone who would appreciate me for having saved that special gift a girl can give only once. I met that guy in college. We've been married for six years, and I couldn't be happier. M. M. IN LITTLE ROCK

DEAR ABBY: I'm writing in reference to "Hurting in Hartford." I want her to know she's not alone. I will turn 20 next month and I'm still a virgin. I plan to stay that way until I'm married. I've had three relationships that ended because I wouldn't have sex.

I'm not a cold fish. I enjoy hugging, kissing and cuddling, but I'm not a tease. I tell them up front how far I'll go. I'm only human, but I never get into a situation I can't handle. Remember, you'll never miss what you haven't had. NOT HURTING IN ENID, OKLAHOMA

*Permission for use of this article, dated Sunday, April 5, 1987, granted by Universal Press Syndicate.

So we ask again the question, *why not?* You are probably aware that in life everything has cause and effect. Simply stated, we reap what we sow. When we do what is good and right, good and right things come of it. Peace, happiness, a sense of security and well-being and self respect are some of what we harvest into our lives when we do the right thing. When we do what is wrong, destruction, heartache, disappointment and sometimes death are the results.

So let's look at the **great chemistry equation of life** when people have out-of-marriage sex. The results are often tragic, long-lasting and irreversible:

outside of marriage   *resulting in*

ABORTION OF mIllIONs OF babies eVERY YEAR

Abortion is murder. There is nothing more helpless and vulnerable than a baby in the womb. So to destroy a precious life because it is inconvenient or shameful to be pregnant is horrendous. I urge you to continue reading this book, because if this is something you have done, very thankfully, you can be forgiven.

BIRTH OF UNWANTED CHIIDREN

The Bible clearly states that children are a gift from God. They are his reward.[1] If a child is unwanted by his mother, very often he is neglected or abused. This is tragic and completely avoidable.

HOmEs sHATTERED By DIvORCE

The foolish man built his house on the sand. When the rain came down and the floods came up, the house on the sand fell flat. But the wise man built his house on the rock. When the rain came down and the floods came up, the house on the rock stood fast.[2]

I will teach you how to build your house on the rock because when the rain and the floods come, I want your house to stand strong.

DEvAsTATING sEXUAlly TRANSMITTED DISEASEs (sTDs)

STDs are devastating, not only physically, but emotionally, mentally and spiritually. They are as avoidable as not eating food that is rotten or jumping off the top of a cliff into the Grand Canyon without a parachute. How and why to avoid this disease trap is part of the gift you'll receive from this book.

DEATH FROm AIDs

As mentioned earlier, we reap what we sow. It is a universal law that is impossible to escape. It is as impossible to escape this law as hitting a tennis ball against a wall and expecting it not to bounce back. So, very tragically, people die from AIDS. It is a very painful and agonizing death that I have personally witnessed when I watched a friend's brother die from it.

sUICIDE

People take their lives when frozen in pain, despair and hopelessness. Sex outside of marriage is a downhill slide. Suicide is a tragedy that never needs to happen in your life. The solution is simple and I urge you to continue reading to discover how great the benefits and blessings are when you live safely inside the circle.

An important question

If you were the master chemist who designed you and everything that exists, are these the results you would want from the equation of a man and woman coming together? Is there a way out? Is there a better way? Is there a way to be truly happy and fulfilled? YES! But first let's talk a little about you. *Who are you really?*

3. The Real you

Are you more than the pretty face in the mirror or the athlete on the field? Are you more than your job description, your ancestry or your salary? Yes, you are.

Your physical body is the container for your real self. Inside you is the real you which is called your inner man.[3] Your inner man (self) is comprised of your spirit and soul (your mind, emotion and will). Therefore, your "self" has three aspects, your body, soul and spirit.[4] These three aspects, or parts of you, were designed to work together to give your life peace and stability.

However, often these three parts are in conflict with one another, competing over which one will direct your life. Have you noticed that this creates conflict, turmoil and confusion?

You may have said to yourself, "My heart told me one thing but my mind, my good sense, told me something else." Or maybe you had a gut level feeling about something but you rationalized it and it ended up getting hurt. These are examples of the soul being in conflict with itself.

Even more serious than this internal tug-of-war is when the soul goes completely dark and the mind, emotion and will agree upon doing what is terribly wrong. At this point, the conscience, the internal bell that sounds an alarm when wrong is chosen over right, no longer functions. It is as if someone put a hot iron to it and destroyed its nerves. Hitler would be an example, as would a murderer.

Is there any way out of this internal tug-of-war or an escape for the soul captured in darkness? Is there a way that these three parts of you can cooperate with each other instead of battling with each other? Is there a way that the most inexcusable human being can come into a place of peace? Can you send stress out the door of your life? *Yes! Please read on.*

4. The master Controller

Just as an airport needs a radio control tower operator to manage flights in and out safely, we also need something that has greater vision than we have to manage our souls.

Just as a computer has a hard drive that manages all the software in it, we also need an internal hard drive that is on our side to empower us to overcome our confusion and inner conflicts.

Just as a dance troupe needs a choreographer to design the dance steps to coordinate the dancers so that they can flow together with beauty and precision, so we need an internal choreographer to coordinate our steps along the path of life.

So what we need is a Master Controller, wouldn't you agree? But what would he have to be like to take on this terrific task? If we were to design a "dream" Master Controller for this job, what would he have to be like in order for you to entrust your real self, your inner man, to him?

First, he would have to be **bigger than our mind emotion and will** in order to rule them well. He would have to have not only the power but the compassion to coordinate them so that harmony could come into our lives.

Second, he would have to **care about us**. It would be disastrous to willingly submit ourselves to a tyrant who would enslave us.

Third, he would have to be someone we could **trust completely** since we're talking about giving him control over everything we are.

Fourth, he would have to be much more **intelligent** than any person on earth in order to handle this job.

Fifth, he would have to **have vision** far and wide and in every direction like the radio control tower operator. And he would have to be able to see as well in the dark as he does in the daytime. He would even have to be able to see into the future!

Sixth, he would have to thoroughly **understand us** because without that intimate knowledge of us he couldn't be personal. That means he would have to understand our deepest motives, thoughts, ambitions, talents, dreams, hopes and fears. *Nothing would be hidden from his data bank of information about who we are-- and that is to our advantage.*

Seventh, he would have to be someone one hundred percent committed to operating for our **good** so he would always bring us the **help** we need when we ask for it.

Eighth, he would have to be someone who would **never leave** the operating tower of our inner man. He would always be at work, twenty-four hours a day, seven days a week and would never leave regardless of the difficulty of his job or lack of reward. Lack of reward would come when we don't acknowledge and appreciate his help.

This is a very tall order. Could such a wonderful person ever exist? Yes! I have great news for you!

This is the good news!
There is just such a Master Controller!

Two thousand years ago God took on the form of man. This God-man was full of grace and truth. He was born in a humble manger in Bethlehem. Once he became thirty years old he began teaching and healing people. He brought heaven to earth and set people free from the bondage inside their souls. Even though he committed no crime whatsoever, he was viciously tortured and hung to die on a cross.

For three days he lay dead in a tomb. But after the third day he came alive from the dead. By rising from the dead he conquered death, hell and the power of the grave.

Many people saw him after he came back to life. After forty days on earth, he rose into the sky and returned to heaven. To this very day, he is seated in heaven praying for us. The day is coming when he will come back to earth to take us home to heaven.

His name is Jesus Christ. He is the one who formed you inside your mother before you were born. He is not only your creator but the creator of everything that is. His power holds everything together.

You may ask, why was a wonderful, powerful, innocent man tortured and killed?

God is absolutely holy and pure. Because we came into this world filthy instead of pure and holy on the inside, something had to be done. During the time of the Old Testament, God told his people to sacrifice animals to atone or wash away the filthiness of their lives. Animals were sacrificed because life itself is in the blood. When they were sacrificed, the people were washed clean of their filthiness. But most of their hearts were like stone and they didn't listen to him.

So you may be wondering, how did people become filthy in the first place?

There was a war in heaven. One of the most beautiful and powerful angels ever, Lucifer, decided he wanted to be God. He rebelled against God and was thrown out of heaven along with a third of the angels he talked into following him.[5]

He was cast to the earth and had the ability to speak to people. Unfortunately, he hated God and lied about the truth.

He lied to the first people God ever made and they listened to his lie. They did exactly what God told them not to do and their rebellion broke their perfect relationship with him.

People were designed to live forever in God's care. But the first people, by their disobedience and rebellion, ruined his perfect plan. Sin entered their lives. Sin means that we "miss the mark." If you've ever shot a bow and arrow and missed the target, that is what we, as humans, do in relation to God.

Satan, the devil, the beautiful angel cast out of heaven, hates God and every human being. He hates us because we are made in God's image. His tactics are to kill, steal, and destroy.[6] He is a liar and the father of lies.[7] Because he ruined the relationship that God had with the first people, everyone to this day comes into life with a broken relationship with God. Instead of knowing and loving God, people are born missing the mark. In other words, everyone is born "in sin."

But you may say, how could a beautiful baby be born in sin? Babies are beautiful because we are made in the image of God. But have you ever seen a two-year-old throw a fit because of his self-will and self-centeredness? Or have you seen someone bully someone because of the jealousy and hatred in his heart? Have you ever seen someone intentionally hurt someone or spend his time thinking of ways to be sneaky about doing something wrong?

These are all examples of the sin that is in us. These are symptoms of the destroyer's ways in us. The devil is the thief and the destroyer. We come into life in the darkness of his evil ways. The devil is our father because of the lie that the first people believed and acted upon.

God gave the commandments in the Old Testament to protect people from the corruption, the sin, within them. His heart was broken when his people refused to honor and obey him. He cried out through his prophets that he wanted to be their God and for them to be his people but they refused to let him be God. They were hard-hearted and stiff-necked and wanted to follow their own selfish ways.[8]

So God finally gave his very own son, Christ himself, as the ultimate sacrifice to pay the way for humanity to come back to him.

God loved us so much that he gave his only son so that whoever believes in him would not perish but have everlasting life.[9]

Jesus' horrific death on the cross was the only way to reconcile humanity back to God's care. Jesus paid the ultimate price, his precious life, so that he could offer us the ultimate gift of forgiveness of our sins and everlasting life with God in his kingdom.

When we accept Jesus into our hearts, God washes away our sin and we become holy and acceptable to him. Then we are translated into another kingdom, God's kingdom. God becomes our Father and Jesus becomes our Savior, brother and friend.[10]

God does this for us because of his great love and mercy. Because of his grace, the unmerited favor he gives us, he washes our sins away. He puts our sins as far as the east is from the west and remembers them no more.[11] They are thrown into the sea of forgetfulness.[12] *Forgiven! Forgotten! Forever!*

When we accept him he looks on us as clean and pure. He's on our side. Our job is to agree with him on everything he declares in his Holy Word about our new standing with him as his precious children and then to act accordingly.

Our life on earth is very short. When we accept that Jesus shed his blood for us, we are cleansed of all our sin, whiter than snow.[13] Then we can live with God forever. His love is unchanging and it lasts forever.

He loves us and will never leave us or forsake us. He fulfills everything we need in a master controller. He is bigger than we can imagine. He cares about us. He is completely trustworthy. His intelligence is what created us and everything that exists. His vision is unlimited because he sees the beginning to the end. He understands us better than we know ourselves. He works for our good because of his great love. He helps us with help far beyond and to a much greater depth than what we could ever access ourselves because of his wholehearted commitment to our good. He never leaves us or forsakes us.

I want to ask you now to accept Jesus and his forgiveness into your heart. You can simply say this prayer and he will answer you:

Dear Lord Jesus,
Thank you for dying on the cross for me to take away all of my sin. Please forgive me. Please come into my heart and wash me white as snow. I give you everything that I am, my mind, emotion, and will. I give you my heart. I want you to have full control of my life. Thank you, dear Jesus. I love you. Amen

Now that you've accepted Jesus into your heart,

there are some things for you to do to maintain this new relationship with your God and your Savior.

First, get a Bible and begin to read it.[14] *Devour it!* I would recommend starting with the book of John in the New Testament. John was one of Jesus' disciples and was his closest friend. The Bible is God's Word and is alive and powerful.[15] As you read it and study it, God will write it on your heart so that you do not sin against him.[16] It addresses every situation we will ever face. It shows us God's reliable, unchangeable character and his amazing power to change and restore our lives. All things are possible with him.[17]

Second, get connected with other believers. They are your new family since everyone who asks Jesus into his heart becomes a child of God. This is important for your growth and security in Christ. Jesus said that his body is the church. So if you're in church, a prayer group, a fellowship group or talking on the phone with another believer, he is right there with you. That is true because he said that if two or more are gathered together in his name, he is among them.[18]

Third, continue to talk with God. He's always there for you. He promises to never leave you or forsake you. He promises to answer you and care for you. He is faithful and true. He is the same today, yesterday and forever[19] and is the Rock you can build your life on that will never fail. Prayer is communication with our Father God through his son, Jesus.

Fourth, tell others about your new life in Christ. It will strengthen your faith and encourage others to accept him as well.

Fifth, every day turn over everything you are to him. He is the dream master controller for your life, even though that is not a term the Bible uses. However, the Bible tells us very plainly how to have him in control of our lives. Just as Jesus was the sacrifice who paid the price for our sin, the Bible tells us to give ourselves to God as a living sacrifice. That means we have to die to our old ways of thinking and going about life. So turn yourself over to him every day and he will do everything he promises to do in your life. Die to yourself and live for him.[20]

In the Bible, Jesus said that we're his sheep and he's our good shepherd.[21] Consciously determine to follow him every day. Listen for his voice to lead you because he will. If you find you want to go your own way, choose his way. Obey his word and his voice. He's the good shepherd that laid his life down for his sheep so he knows the best way for you to go.[22]

The Lord is always a gentleman. He honors our will and when we willingly give ourselves to him, we give him permission to do his work in us. His intent is to heal us and to free us from everything that captures and entangles us.[23]

The Bible says that he came to heal the broken-hearted and save the crushed in spirit.[24] There is nothing too difficult for him to accomplish. He can do above and beyond what we can ask or think.[25] His ways are above our ways and his thoughts are above our thoughts.[26]

So you now have a new life. Your sins are as far away from you as the east is from the west.[27] You are a new creation in him.[28] You have been born again.[29] You now have a Heavenly Father. Your name is written on the palm of his hand. You're always on his mind.[30] You have a Savior who died for you. Now I want to tell you about one more aspect to this wonderful new life you have been given.

5. spirit Control Room

One day a five-year-old asked me how Jesus could live inside us since he's a man. I thought it was a good question.

There's another place inside us called our "spirit." So when we invite Jesus into our hearts, he lives in our spirit with his Holy Spirit. Jesus was filled with the Spirit of God, the Holy Spirit. Because he was filled with the Spirit, he was able to do everything that God the Father showed him to do. He healed the sick, raised the dead, cast out demons and cleansed the lepers.[31,32] He taught thousands of people the truth and declared the good news about the kingdom of God.

The very same Spirit that filled Jesus is the Spirit that comes into our spirits when we accept him into our hearts. Jesus said that his plan for us is that we do the same things that he did when he was on earth but in greater measure.[33] That is reasonable because he is the head of the church and we're his body. If we, the body of Christ, are not filled with the same thing that Christ, the head, is filled with, the two would not be compatible or work together properly.

For that reason, we need to be filled with the same Spirit that filled Jesus. The Bible talks about this in the book of John. The book of John was written by one of Jesus' disciples. However, what we're about to discuss has to do with another John, John the Baptist, who was Jesus' cousin.

He was sent by God to prepare people's hearts for Jesus to come to be their Lord and Savior. He had been baptizing people in the river after they had turned away from their sins.

John declared, *"I baptize with water, but there is someone standing among you who you don't know. I'm not even worthy to untie his shoes."*[34]

The next day John saw Jesus coming toward him and said, "Look, the Lamb of God, who takes away the sin of the world! This is the one I meant when I said, 'A man who comes after me has surpassed me because he was before me.' I did not know him myself, but the reason I have been baptizing with water was to make a way so that he could be revealed to Israel."[35]

Then John gave this testimony: "I saw the Spirit come down from heaven as a dove and land on Jesus. He stayed on him. I wouldn't have known him except that the one who sent me to baptize with water told me, 'The man on whom you see the Spirit come down and remain is he who will baptize with the Holy Spirit.' I have seen and testify that this is the Son of God."[36]

In the book of Luke, another of Jesus' disciples, people wanted John to tell them if he, John, were the Christ. *Again he told them, "I baptize* with water but someone much mightier than I am is coming and I'm not worthy to even untie his shoes. He will baptize you with the Holy Spirit (or Holy Ghost) and with fire."[37]

What does "baptize" mean? It means "to make something completely wet, to overwhelm it with water, to submerge or to wash it." It is the difference between just putting our toe in the water or wading in up to our knees and diving in. Jesus wants us to be completely filled with His Spirit.

Jesus wants us to be baptized in the Holy Spirit because our job is to do the same things he did. Because of that, we need the same power from the same Spirit he had.

Just the way that soldiers are commissioned to do their job in the army, Jesus told us what to do:

Jesus said, "All power is given to me in heaven and in earth."[38]

"Jesus also said, 'Go everywhere in the world, and preach the gospel (good news) to every creature. He that believes and is baptized shall be saved. He that doesn't believe will be damned.

And these signs shall follow them that believe: In my name they shall cast out devils. They shall speak with new tongues. They shall take up serpents, and if they drink any deadly thing, it shall not hurt them. They shall lay hands on the sick, and they shall recover.'

After the Lord had spoken these words to them, he was received up into heaven and sat down at the right hand of God.

His disciples obeyed him and preached everywhere, the Lord working with them, and his word was confirmed with signs following them."[39]

So it only makes sense that to do a job you have to have the power to do it. By asking Jesus to baptize you in the Holy Spirit, you are asking him to give you that power.

One of the major functions Jesus has in our lives is to baptize us in the Holy Spirit. We know how major this is because it is recounted in three of the four gospels with almost the same wording. You can read these accounts in Matthew 3:11, Mark 1:7-8 and John 1:33.

Jesus' followers in the early church were instructed to wait in the upper room until the Holy Spirit came to them. This is recorded in the second chapter of Acts. *"And when the day of Pentecost had come, they were all together in one place. And suddenly there came from heaven a noise like a violent, rushing wind, and it filled the whole house where they were sitting. And there appeared to them tongues as of fire distributing themselves, and they rested on each of them. And they were all filled with the Holy Spirit and began to speak with other tongues, as the Spirit was giving them utterance."* Acts 2:1-4 New American Standard Version.

One of the signs that follow Jesus' believers in the verse from Mark chapter 16 is that they will speak in "new tongues." This is a language that we don't learn but is given to us as a very useful gift. If we're in a group, God can speak through us in our new language (sometimes called a "prayer language") and someone else can interpret it in the group. If it is not interpreted, it is not useful to the group. If we're alone we can sing, pray or pray silently in our language. Its purpose is to build up (edify) our spirits because it is the Spirit of God in us praying, speaking or singing. The spirit of God is the architect and house builder who is building us up into a beautiful temple, His holy habitation. You can learn more about this in the Bible in the book of First Corinthians chapter 14, verses 2 through 4.

To receive the baptism in the Holy Spirit with the gift of speaking in tongues, simply pray:

Dear Jesus, please baptize me in your Holy Spirit and give me the gift of speaking in tongues so that I can build up my spirit and do your will. Thank you that you are faithful and thank you for answering my prayer. Amen

To facilitate this prayer simply open your mouth and Jesus will give you utterance in another language.

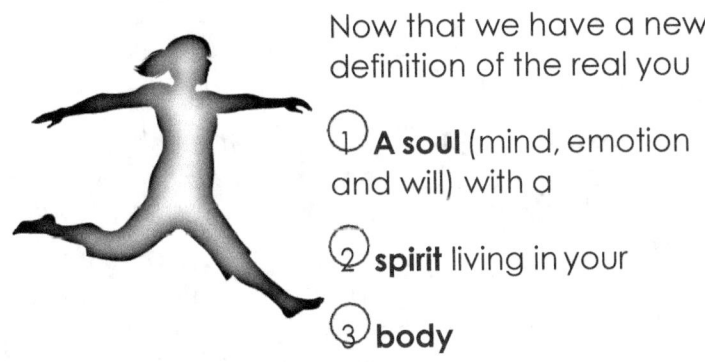

Now that we have a new definition of the real you

① **A soul** (mind, emotion and will) with a

② **spirit** living in your

③ **body**

we can discuss why to save sex for marriage with a whole, new understanding.

6. But It's Too late!

You may be thinking right now. "Forget it. I've already blown it. It's too late for me!"

This is where the incredibly wonderful, good news about our God who is love according to 1 John 4:16b comes in.

Have you ever been to the beach and built a sand castle or written your name in the sand?

Not long afterward, the tide came in and washed it all away and made the beach look as if no one had ever touched it.

That is exactly what God does with our lives when we've blown it and ask him to forgive us and restore us. There are no limits to his ability to forgive. And he is no garbage picker. He will not resurrect your sin and put it in your face again. He throws that sin as far away as the east is from the west. He just asks that we turn away from it and not repeat it.

7. The Original Design

Before looking at the reasons why sex outside of marriage should absolutely be avoided, let's look first at the

Original Design

intended by our magnificent Creator for sex.

First, since we know that the Word of God, the Bible, is true, we take as fact that God created man and woman, blessed them and gave them authority over his creation.

God said, "Let us make man in our image, after our likeness, and let them have dominion (power) over the fish of the sea, and over the fowl of the air, and over the cattle, and over all the earth, and over every creeping thing that is on the earth.

So God created man in his own image, in the image of God he created them. He created them male and female." [40]

Second, God made man <u>and</u> woman because it wasn't good for man to be alone.

And the Lord God said, "It is not good that man should be alone. I will make him a helper comparable (worthy of comparison) to him. [41] *Then God made the man fall into a deep sleep. And while he was asleep, he took out one of his ribs and closed his flesh back up. God fashioned the rib he had taken from the man into a woman and brought her to the man.*

And the man said, "This is bone of my bones and flesh of my flesh. She is to be called Woman, because she was taken from Man."

Therefore, a man shall leave his father and his mother and shall cleave (be glued to) his wife and they shall be one flesh. And they were both naked, the man and his wife, and they were not ashamed.[42]

YES! $1+1=1$

So now we have seen our magnificent God of Love do a beautiful thing. He created a man in his image and from him created his partner, a woman, who was perfect for him. He "blessed" them, which means, he bestowed on them everything that would make them happy.

If you had just created a man and woman who you wanted to be happy, what would you do next?

Let's look at what earthly parents do. Do you remember when you were a lot younger? Hopefully your parents didn't want you to play in the street because of the danger of being hit by a car. They wouldn't let you play with matches. They warned you not to take rides with strangers. They wanted you to eat your vegetables and to get to bed on time. In other words, they gave you rules to protect you.

Maybe about now you're shouting, "Wait! Nobody ever cared about me! No one gave me any rules! I just did whatever I wanted! And I'm not about to get stuck with a bunch of rules now!"

If that's the case, whoever raised you, failed you. Please forgive them. They did the best they could with where they were in their lives. Remember, we all come into life in sin. But now you have a new father, your Heavenly Father, who loves you. All his rules are in your very best interest for your happiness. And remember, too, we have to forgive or we are not forgiven.[43] Jesus gave his life for us through a horrible death so that we could be forgiven and make us new creatures in him with a new heart.

So if that is what your heart is crying out, ask the Lord to heal your broken heart and to enable you to forgive those who let you down and failed you.

8. Rules for the Good life

What are some of God's rules to keep us inside his circle of safety and to keep our lives upright?

DO NOT COmmIT ADULTERy

After Satan came in and polluted God's creation with sin and rebellion, God's heart yearned to keep us safe within his arms of love.

Because marriage and sexual union are so precious and the consequences of violating that union are so devastating, God, in his wisdom and love, set down absolute rules to protect his beloved creation.

This was so critical to our well-being that he carved his commandments into stone.

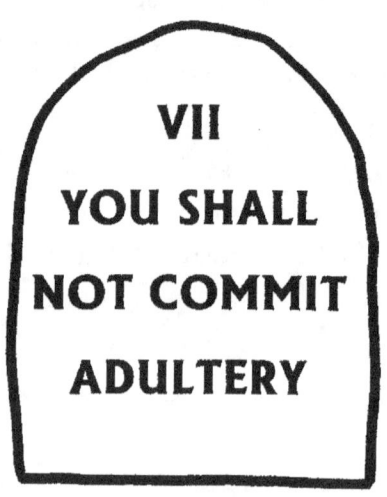

Exodus 20:14

What does this commandment tell us about God's heart for us?

"Oh, that they had such a heart in them that they would fear (respect) me and keep all my commandments always, that it might be well with them, and with their children forever!"[44]

God gives his commandments to protect us so that things would be well with us. His Father's heart warns us, "Beware! I don't want you hurt!" He wants to protect us just as a mother hen nestles her chicks under her wing of warmth and comfort. *"For you have been a shelter for me, and a strong tower from the enemy. I will live in your tabernacle (home or tent) forever; I will trust in the shelter of your wings."*[45]

God is the giver of every good and perfect gift.[46] He vehemently forbids sex outside of marriage because instead of being a good and perfect gift, it brings tragedy and destruction because it is sin. It is from the hand of the evil one, the tyrant who enslaves.

sTAy AWAy FROm sEXUaL IMMorALiTY

"You should abstain (completely stay away from) fornication (sex between two unmarried people) because this is God's will and your sanctification (that which sets you apart as God's own). You should know how to possess your vessel (control your body) in sanctification (being set apart for Him) and honor. Not in the lust (passion, inappropriate affection) of concupiscence (a longing for what is forbidden), being just like the people who don't know God....for God has not called us to uncleanness but to holiness."[47]

FLEE yOUTHFuL LUsTs

"Also flee (break free and run for your life from) youthful lusts, but seek after righteousness (having right standing with God and other people), faith, charity (love) and peace with those people who call on the Lord out of a pure heart."[48]

KEEP yOURsELF PURE

"Beloved one, right now we are the sons of God and it hasn't appeared to us yet what we shall be, but we know we shall be like him (Jesus) because we shall see him as he is. Everyone who has this hope in him (of becoming like Jesus) purifies himself, just as he is pure (absolutely sinless)."[49]

Our job is to listen to these warnings and commandments and warnings and make sure our lives line up with them. The next part of this book will give you ten good reasons why this is the right way to live your life.

PART TWO: TEN GOOD REASONS TO SAY "NO" TO SEX OUTSIDE OF MARRIAGE

1. Oneness with Christ

God has called us to be joined to Christ as our beloved bridegroom. Once we become his, we also become the temple of the Holy Ghost, or Holy Spirit.[50]

Marriage, symbolic of our relationship with Christ, is a union to be highly esteemed and valued. It is truly of the highest order. This is true to such a degree that Jesus' beloved church, his body, is *his bride.*

You might be thinking, "Whoa!! I'm a guy, not a girl! How in the world could I be the 'Bride of Christ'?"

In the Spirit, there is neither male nor female.[51] When Christ comes into us, he becomes one with us. This is a marvelous and mystical union.

We get a glimpse of Jesus' bride in the book of Revelation where the bride is called the "New Jerusalem." *This city does not need the sun or moon to shine on it, because the glory of God gives it light and the Lamb (Jesus Christ) is its lamp."*[52]

The glorious news is that whether you are a man or woman, you are chosen to be the bride of Jesus Christ. *Jesus is returning for a glorious church, his bride, that is holy and blameless without a stain or wrinkle or any other blemish.*[53]

But the legacy for the fearful (cowards), the unbelieving, the vile who worship obscenities, for murderers and the sexually immoral, and for those who practice magic arts, worshippers of false gods and all liars—their place will be in the fiery lake of burning sulfur. This is the second death."[54]

One of the seven angels showed John the Bride of Christ, the New Jerusalem, coming down out of heaven. It had the glory of God and her light was like a most precious stone...[55]

We are a bride with a future—a plan and a purpose from God Himself. We are made to be one with (married to) Jesus Christ. "Jesus will never forsake us but returns to receive us as his chaste virgin, his bride."[56]

After the marriage supper of the Lamb, our purpose begins to unfold even more. "To him who loves us and has washed away our sins with his blood, and made us kings and priests to God and his Father, be glory and dominion forever and ever. Amen!"[57]

So, "if we persevere (remain determined to the end), then we shall reign with Him."[58]

What a future we have! To reign and rule with Christ himself as his beloved bride!

What this means is that we're intended to have the blessing of

DOUBLE UNITY

With Christ: "We are members of his body, of his flesh and of his bones."[59]

In Marriage: "*For this reason a man shall leave his father and mother and be joined to his wife and the two shall become one flesh.*"[60]

So suddenly this mystical union of two becoming one is far beyond a physical act. It is a holy estate and commitment, one deeply expressive of the full and never ending love that Jesus proclaims—that his believers, the church, are his beautiful bride.

2. It is Wrong!

All of God's commandments were given out of a heart that longs to protect us. This is his warning: *FLEE FORNICATION!* Fornication is voluntary sex between unmarried persons.

All other sins that someone may commit are done outside the body, but a sexually immoral person <u>sins against his own body</u>.[61]

"*Do you not realize that your body is the temple of the Holy Spirit, who you received from God? You are not your own property. You have been bought with a price (Jesus shedding his blood on the cross for you), so glorify God in your body and in your spirit, which are God's.*"[62]

When we choose to go our own way and violate God's commandments, we are wrong and pay the consequences, sometimes finding ourselves as unprotected as orphans on the street.

FACT: All of nature's forces can either save or destroy lives. A cool drink of water in the desert could save a life. Rushing torrents of water overflowing the banks of a river often destroy lives and property. Fire, too, can bring comfort when one is cold and in the darkness of a wilderness. And yet, an uncontrolled raging fire often brings pain, terrible death and destruction.

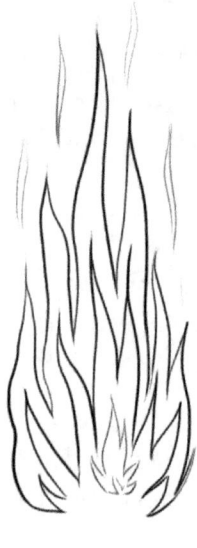

This is also true with the fire of sex, one of God's most beautiful and cherished gifts. The fire of sexual union can warm and heal a marriage. He is the giver of every good and perfect gift.

Who would know better how to use his gift to bring the greatest blessing into our lives than he who created the gift?

Outside of marriage, however, the same fire, when uncontrolled, can burn and destroy acres of homes and families. It often brings division instead of unity, tearing families apart and reaping chaos and destruction.

Destruction of homes and families is wrong. It is a federal spiritual offense.

Be wise and protect yourself, God's precious possession. You now have a Heavenly Father who is faithful and trustworthy. Trust his wisdom in urging you to value yourself and maintain your purity. He does love you.

3. *It is a Counterfeit*

Sex outside of marriage is a counterfeit to true intimacy, a cheap imitation of the beautiful gift it is meant to be. Ask any couple who has been married for several years how long it has taken for them to really get to know each other. Some may tell you that after fifty years of marriage, they are still discovering intricacies about each other.

True intimacy is founded on respect and genuine interest in another person's ideas, hopes, dreams, beliefs, concerns, feelings and experiences.

This kind of closeness is cultivated with honesty and openness. It begins in the spirit and grows into the soul, the mind, emotion and will. Healthy intimacy happens when people feel safe, accepted and comfortable. It is the kind of intimacy that lets us laugh and cry and talk forever with someone with whom we feel close.

But when sex is allowed outside the circle of safety, which maintains true intimacy, the aftermath is often guilt, emptiness, lack of connection, feelings of being used or deceived and abandoned.

When we take the time to build genuine closeness, we are rewarded with friendships that are precious and long lasting. Our creator tells us to "flee youthful lusts" for the good purpose of protecting us so that we can make room for healthy and rewarding relationships to develop.

Satan, the father of lies, appears as an angel of light.[63]

WATCH OUT FOR HIS TRICKS!

Stick to the straight and narrow Word of God.
Live smart. Stay safe. Keep your life upright.
Remember to just go home when you're tired!

4. *It Tears Us Apart*

Something mystical happens in sexual union. Two become one. After the Lord created Eve and gave her to Adam, the Bible explains, *"A man shall leave his father and mother and be joined to (glued to) his wife, and they shall become one flesh."*[64]

Sexual union in marriage is valuable. However, this same union, this blending of spirits and bodies into one, takes place whether the union is ordained through marriage or is a one-night stand.

In marriage, the union is meant to be nurtured and supported through love, commitment and faithfulness.

In a one-night stand, the partner's spirit remains mingled with ours, even though the person has walked out the door. Because of this mingling, a person is literally "torn apart" by desertion since he has become "one flesh" with that partner.

This can happen over and over if someone has multiple sexual encounters, leaving that person mingled with the spirits of many people. Multiple partners can cause a lot of torment, confusion, and fragmentation. Therefore, it's important to get rid of the spirits of any sexual partners by saying this simple prayer.

You may want someone else to agree with you as you pray this prayer. As Jesus said, *"In truth I tell you, whatever you bind on earth will be bound in heaven; whatever you loose on earth will be loosed in heaven. In truth I tell you once again, if two of you on earth agree as touching anything that they shall ask, it will be done for them by my Father who is in heaven. For where two or three are gathered together in my name, I am there among them."*[65]

Praying this prayer is a golden opportunity to get help from the one who made us, loves us, frees us and restores us!

Lord Jesus, please forgive me for my sexual   I take authority over the spirits of___, ___, ___ (names of partners) and command them to leave me now in your name. Thank you, Lord, for cleansing me of these spirits. Holy Spirit, fill me with your Spirit and with your love. Thank you. In Jesus' Name. Amen

5. It is Degrading

There is far more of you to get to know than your body, the shell in which you live. To take "you" without exploring and valuing your mind, values, attitudes and experiences is an insult to you!

Give yourself permission to be that many faceted treasures that will take time to value and appreciate. Even in an age of instant everything, you have the right <u>not</u> to be instant!

Respect yourself and others will respect you. Don't be left empty and alone. Instead, put on the righteousness of Christ and you will be blessed. What comes with this word "blessed" is powerful. In the Greek, it means "to be thought well of, praised, adored, fortunate and happy."

You have a great life to live- one blessed by the Lord!

6. It is Robbery

For a man to take a woman's body as he would a wife without the commitment of marriage is robbing from her and from the Lord. As a believer, she is not her own; she belongs to the one who purchased her through his death.[66] That is as high a price as anyone could ever pay. There is no greater love than this, that a man lays down his life for his friends.[67]

In addition, it still stands true. God is a jealous God. [68]

Only a husband has the right to delight in his wife, not someone who has no commitment to her and has not come into her life through the door of marriage.

God has placed us inside a wonderful circle of safety. He's given us first class protection through his warnings and clear directions.

7. It Violates the Child-like Part of Us

We all know that we need love. Expressions of love that show warmth, caring, affection and nurturing are vital and wonderful for our health and well-being.

Shockingly, babies that are cared for physically but not held and cuddled sometimes actually die.

So we as children, teenagers and adults need affection to be healthy. Natural and positive, healthy affection heals, calms, soothes, restores and builds trust. It is given with respect, kindness, gentleness and consideration, leaving the one receiving the affection feeling safe and protected.

This affection happens inside a safe yard with a fence around it, protected from harm. But what happens when someone climbs over the fence and gets into sexual behavior of any kind? *Violation.*

The sacred trust of this safe and nurturing relationship is broken. Its sweetness and wholesomeness vanish. And then confusion sets in because those sexual acts that "feel good" on one level, are devastating on a deeper level, where they register as abuse and disrespect.

And then come upset feelings, arguments, insecurity and possessiveness, all because two people didn't stay inside the circle of safety, honoring the rules laid down for their protection.

So often we hear the phrase "consenting adults." Yes, perhaps "consenting adults" in chronological age, but still like children on another level.

Why else would so many polls show that women would often rather be held and treated tenderly than have sex?

A man is responsible to recognize his position of strength and that he is the head of the relationship. He is to use his strength and understanding to protect and care for the woman in his life, vowing to never prey upon her vulnerability. His job is to protect her from her own sexuality.

8. *It is A Faithless Act*

There are two standards we have to look at:

One is the standard of the world that tells us, "You had better be sure that you are sexually compatible. You had better try him or her out." *The Bible says that a wicked and adulterous generation demands a sign.*[69] In this case, the demand is for a sign of adequate sexual performance. This demand is profoundly self-centered. This is the truth: *"Whatever is not of faith is sin."*[70]

To "test someone out" is sin because it is not trusting that God, the giver of every good and perfect gift, will give us the right mate and will put this confidence in our hearts and spirits.

The other standard is the one God establishes, to keep ourselves untouched.

It is a violation of another person's dignity and self-respect to disregard God's standard. How can people expect God's fullest blessing when they build a relationship built on violation? Our only way of escape is to accept God's forgiveness. He's in the business of transforming our lives and healing the past when we give our lives to him.

The devil has promoted a treacherous and deceptive lie that reaps heartache, confusion, bondage and children without two parents to raise them when we fall into the trap of testing someone out. This is clearly *Satan appearing as an angel of light.*[71] Beware of his deception designed to entrap you and then devour you.

What a sharp contrast to the One who brings joy, vision, freedom and security when we obey his commandments!!

9. *We May Marry the Wrong Person*

When two people are attracted to each other, often the attraction starts with the physical. If the physical aspect has no restraint, then the lust of the flesh goes into full swing. Result? "Falling in love" and the resultant blindness to what might be deadly character flaws in the other person. These flaws are often either overlooked or not seen at all because of the power of the flesh and the sexual union.

The flesh can easily tell someone "this is the one." If that person rushes headlong into marriage, he may soon discover after the passion has cooled off, that he's married to a stranger. Sometimes he can get to know the stranger he is with, but often he's trapped in a life of quiet desperation.

It would only seem reasonable that if someone is "with" another person physically that he would also have intimacy with that person's mind, emotion, heart and soul. Not the case.

This scenario is one of Satan's favorite tactics to confuse and destroy lives. He uses the heightened feelings that sex brings to smoke screen what is really going on. He blinds the heart and confuses the mind with the misuse of one of God's best gifts.

So to avoid marrying a stranger, just say "no" to sex outside of marriage.

Some suggestions: Get to know each other as human beings. Ask questions. Laugh together. Become best friends. Develop trust. Help each other out. Pray for each other. Put a ring on your wedding ring finger that reminds you that you are the bride of Christ and are saving yourself for whomever the Lord has for you.

Then you will be on solid ground when considering giving everything you are, including your family and finances, to someone else for the rest of your life.

You are your most valuable and prized asset. Don't give yourself easily or lightly to anyone. Let your Father in heaven be completely involved in your love life. He has the best in store for you.

10. It Has Tragic Consequences

Good fruit comes from good trees. If an idea is good, then it will have good results. It will bear good fruit.[72] Sex outside of marriage does not bear good fruit. Instead, it very often produces tragic consequences. These were presented at the beginning of the book: AIDS, STDs (sexually transmitted diseases), abortion (murder) of babies, unwanted and neglected children, divorce and suicide.

Each of these devastating results has the same root cause, the sin of sex outside of sanctified marriage. We do reap what we sow. It is inescapable and far-reaching.

Sow your life inside the circle of safety. Encourage your friends to do the same. Start a tsunami of right thinking and godly action among the people you know. Watch their lives change as they see the favor of God in your life. You will reap happiness and blessing on yourself and many others. Finish strong in the Lord.

PART THREE: PRAyER AnD BLEssInG

Dear Friend,

Earlier in this book, you may have prayed to accept Jesus Christ as your Lord and Savior. That is the most important decision you will ever make. I would like to pray for you now. Please put your name in the blank as we agree together in prayer for you according to Matthew 18:19.

Dearest Heavenly Father,
Thank you for and for his or her decision to accept Jesus into his or her heart. Father, thank you that because of Jesus dying for each of us, our sins are entirely forgiven and forgotten by you.[73,74,75]

Thank you that he or she is now a member of the Kingdom of God and accepted into Christ and into your family.[76]

Lord, I ask for a very special blessing upon this person, that he or she would be anointed to receive a love for the Bible, the living Word, so that he or she will be nourished and sustained by it and that it would be the joy and rejoicing of his or her heart.[77, 78]

Impart to him or her "the truth that sets him or her free." [79]

I pray also, Father, for this person in the sexual realm. I ask that you would forgive him or her for wandering into territory that has caused him or her pain and heartache, if this were the case.[80]

*I ask that you bind up his or her broken heart[81]
and renew a right spirit within him or her.[82] I also
take authority over any spirits that have attached
themselves to this person's spirit and I command
these spirits to leave in the Name of Jesus.[83] I also
ask that if_____is married that you would
bring salvation to his or her spouse.*

*We claim this soul for your kingdom and ask that
there would unity of the Spirit in the bond of peace
between this husband and wife.[84]*

*We also pray that any children that this couple
may have in the future be cleansed by your
Blood and brought to salvation.[85]*

*We cover this precious one now in the Blood of
Christ that sets us free from all sin, guilt and
power of the evil one.*

*If this person has had any other involvement with
Satan's work (occult, witchcraft, habitual lying
or unfaithfulness), I now pray, in agreement with
_____, that he or she now repents of (turns
away from) his or her involvement with these
things of darkness. We cast them far from him or
her and command them to never come back into
his or her life.[86]*

*Thank you, Father, for honoring his or her repentance
and cleansing_____from all these sins. We pray
for a filling of the Holy Spirit in Jesus' Name.
Jesus, thank you for_____and for your great
love for him or her.[87]*

*We ask you, as the one who baptizes in the Holy
Spirit, to baptize_____now and completely fill*

him or her with your Holy Spirit and with fire.[88]
Thank you that the Holy Spirit is our Teacher and Comforter.[89]

Please give _____ the spirit of wisdom and revelation in the knowledge of you[90] *and reveal to_____ his or her spiritual gifts.*[91]

We know we are not made to be alone, so please direct_____ to a church where your Gospel is preached, where your Word, the Bible, is lived and taught, and where people love and accept one another.[92]

I pray that all of_____ 's needs be met, whether they are spiritual, physical, mental, emotional or financial. Please let him or her "prosper and be in health, even as his or her soul prospers."[93]

And Father, if this dear one is single and desires to be married, please prepare this precious heart for the one you have chosen for him or her and bring them together in your perfect way and timing.[94, 95]

Dear Father, thank you for hearing and answering our prayer.[96]

Father, please keep_____ from temptation.[97] *Please become the hiding place for this precious child and surround him or her with songs of deliverance.*[98] *and reveal the length, the depth and the height of your great love to him or her.*[99]

We thank you, too, Father, that you have a plan for_____ 's life, since he or she is your workmanship, created in Christ Jesus to do good works which you prepared in advance for him or her to do.[100] *Reveal your plan to_____ 's heart so that his or* her life will be fully satisfied.

Set him or her free from all fear. By faith we replace the spirit of fear with the "spirit of power, love and a sound mind."[101] And, Satan, your tactics of destruction have been exposed and you are bound and cast out of_'s life in every way.[102]

Praise you, Father, that_____is now a new creature in Christ Jesus, that old things have passed away and that all things have become new.[103]

Father, we bless you and thank you that you have blessed _____ with every spiritual blessings in heavenly places in Christ Jesus.[104] Reveal yourself and your love in mighty ways to_____and give _____ the liberty to share this great treasure of salvation with others. And finally, Father God, thank you for your great faithfulness, that truly you will never leave us or forsake us.[105, 106]

Jesus, prepare this precious one for your glorious return![107]
Praise your Holy Name! Amen

God bless you always.

Your friend,
Christine Lauren

Heartbreak Prevention Quiz

A Pre-Marriage Quiz designed to give you a fresh perspective before writing history on your wedding day.

Dear Friend,

I offer this Heartbreak Prevention Quiz to you to help you measure the quality of your relationship. Answer each question honestly and record your first response with a plus (+) or minus (-) in the box on the left. If a question does not apply to you, put a slash (/) in the box.

☐ Do you really like to be with the person you're going to marry?

☐ If there could be no physical aspect to your relationship, would you still pick this person as your favorite person to be with?

☐ Have the things you've done with this person been things you've been proud of rather than things that violated your conscience or belief system?

☐ Do you genuinely feel that this person respects you and your decisions?

☐ When you talk together, does this person ask you how you think and feel about things?

☐ Does this person have at least five qualities you would want your children to have?

☐ Does this person take the time to listen to your answer after asking you a question?

☐ If you were physically injured before you were married, do you feel this person would still want to marry you?

☐ If this person were not of the opposite sex, would you want him or her as your best friend?

☐ If a crisis struck your life, would this be the first person you would want to be with you?

☐ When one of your parents passes away, will this person be able to love and comfort you?

☐ Does this person encourage you to continue doing the things you enjoy?

☐ Has this person shown respect for you by respecting your body?

☐ When you have argued, does this person keep his or her temper as opposed to hitting you or verbally attacking you?

☐ Does this person like and include your friends in your life together?

☐ If you have ever been sick during your relationship, has this person been compassionate toward you and cared for you?

☐ If you have something to do, does this person volunteer to help you?

☐ Does this person offer support and good suggestions to you when you're struggling to make a decision or to understand something?

☐ If you have ever been deeply upset, was this person willing and able to comfort you and guide you?

☐ Do you feel this person is equal to you mentally, emotionally and spiritually?

☐ If you needed a kidney transplant and only this person could supply it, would he or she?

☐ Is being together more important than always doing things together?

☐Can you talk freely together about each others' dreams and ambitions?

☐ Has this person ever asked you about your childhood?

☐ If you are warm and affectionate, does he or she return your warmth and affection?

☐ Does this person show that he or she accepts and respects your family members?

☐ Can this person keep a secret?

☐ Does this person show respect for your mother and include her graciously in your wedding plans?

☐ Would this person be willing to take either or both of your parents into your home after you're married to live with you if necessary?

☐ Has this person thoughtfully considered your father, mother, sisters and brothers and other family members in your wedding plans?

☐ Do you share the same faith?

☐ Are your lifestyles compatible?

☐ If you do not share the same faith, does this person encourage you to attend your church or synagogue?

☐ Do you have a way to share your spirituality together?

☐ Does this person cheer you up when you need it?

☐ If ever in a tight spot, could you trust this person's judgment?

☐ If there could be no sex between you (it does happen) would you want to marry this person?

☐ If you ever argued with this person, was the issue settled peaceably?

☐ Would this person make a good business partner for you?

☐ If you feel this person is stronger than you are in any way, does he or she use that strength kindly in relation to you?

☐ Is this person supportive when you want to spend time privately with your friends or family?

☐ Do you have as much fun with this person as with your best friend when you were growing up?

☐ Do you sense you could safely trust this person with every part of your life?

☐ Do you respect this person's opinions and seek them out?

☐ If marooned on a desert island, would this person be your companion of choice?

☐ If you had no money to spend to go out, would you still have a good time together?

☐ Does this person have a genuine sense of humor?

☐ Will this person listen to suggestions from you in regard to his or her life?

☐ If his or her habits were your habits, would you be comfortable with yourself?

☐ Does this person enhance your sense of self-worth, self-esteem, and well-being?

☐ Do you see eye to eye as to how to handle your finances?

☐ If it weren't for any pressure to get married, do you really feel you would marry this person?

☐ If you are thirty or over, would this person absolutely be the person you would choose if you were younger?

☐ Do you feel comfortable with whoever seems to be in control of your relationship?

☐ Is this person a good role model for others?

☐ Are your families compatible and supportive of your being together?

☐ Does this person like you for yourself, rather than liking you for what you have or what you do?

☐ Is the person you want to marry legitimately single?

☐ Are you ready to make a commitment to this person for the rest of your life even if you "fall out of love" after you're married?

☐ If the person you want to marry has children, do you genuinely feel the children accept you in a parental role?

☐ If the one you are considering marrying has children, do you consider the children a positive addition to your relationship?

☐ Do you feel the children are ready and willing to receive you in the role of a new parent if your partner has children or vice versa?

☐ Do you agree as to the discipline and upbringing of children?

☐ Do you feel that the person you're considering marrying supports you in developing your talents and abilities?

☐ Does this person teach you good things?

☐ It is said that someone's character can be told by how he or she treats children and animals. Does this person have good character?

☐ Do you feel this person wants to marry you for yourself rather than for the money you or your family has?

☐ Are you choosing to marry freely without feeling pressured or coerced into this decision either externally or internally?

☐ Are you marrying out of your own free will and not to meet the expectations or demands or others, or to please or prove something to someone else?

☐ Do you see eye to eye on how neat a house needs to be kept to be comfortable?

☐ Is this person interesting enough that you ask questions about his or her life?

☐ Are you aware that things don't always work out just because you are getting married?

☐ Do you feel you have consciously listened to your intuition and judgment in making this decision?

☐ Have you consciously taken into account both the encouragement and warning others may have given you about this relationship?

☐ Do you feel that in day-to-day life you will be a priority in this person's life?

☐ Do you both have approximately the same level of health consciousness and maintenance?

☐ Are you sure this person is the sex he or she claims to be?

☐ Are you marrying this person wholeheartedly rather than on the rebound from another relationship?

☐ Do you accept this person as he or she is rather than having a lot of things you would like to change?

☐ After sincerely answering this quiz, would you continue with your wedding plans?

Now let's tally your score:

Take the total number of points (80) and subtract the number of questions that were not applicable (those with a slash mark). This gives you your **adjusted total**.

Original total   80
Number questions not applicable   _____

Adjusted total   =
                                                        _____

Next take the number of positive responses you had on the quiz and divide it by the adjusted total.

For example, if you had 65 positive responses out of a total of 75, divide 65 by 75.

$\frac{65}{75}$ **equals .87 or 87%**

So your final score is_____percent.

To those who have taken this quiz:

Dear Friend,
Marriage can provide the richest and most meaningful relationship possible between two people. If the bulk of your questions had a positive response, the boat of your marriage you're about to step into should float well. You've found someone with quality and character that will stand by you through the years. You are starting with a good foundation and your life together should be happy.

If some of your answers came with a negative reply form you, your boat has some leaks. Leaks can be fixed with prayer, mutual effort, and a desire to change, but it is important to look them squarely in the face before marriage. People typically don't change substantially after marriage.

If many of the answers came with a "no" response from you, please reconsider your decision. I'm sure you know that when a marriage sinks, the consequences are painful and far-reaching... broken hearts, children left without a parent, scars of rejection, mental and emotional anguish. There are no unscathed survivors. So if it appears questionable in any way for you to marry at this time, please reconsider.

Outside of accepting Jesus as your Lord and Savior, marriage is the biggest decision you will ever make. You have all the time in the world, ro matter how old you are today. After all, you are considering investing your heart, your mind, your emotions, your energy, your will and your finances into another person for the rest of your life.

This person needs to be worthy of all that you are. In carpentry, the rule is, "Measure twice; cut once." Measure your relationship. Be sure that cut you are about to make is the one you really want. This is a momentous decision. Once the cut is made, it cannot be undone. Make it with much thought, prayer and with both ears open to both the warnings and encouragement of others.

Please know that even at this possibly late date, you are free to say either "yes" or "no." Even if you have said "yes" but inside you know it was the wrong response for your heart, you can change it now. That word is only a line on a blueprint at this point in time. Change it now, if you know it's in your best interest, before years of anguish bring it crumbling to the ground. The rest of your life is far more important than upsetting or offending a few people now.

It takes courage to listen to your intuition and judgment and to challenge yourself regarding decision that involves your heart so deeply. I wish for you that kind of courage; it pays big dividends. It could save you from falling into the trap of an unhappy or incompatible marriage.

My hope is that you have found this quiz both challenging and stimulating. May the history you write with your life be a joyful account unmarred by the pain and scars brought on by an irreversible decision.

If you feel, after having taken this quiz, that it would be best to wait before making such a serious commitment, remember that you are a wonderful and worthwhile person. You are full of talents and abilities, some perhaps undiscovered and untapped.

Get to know yourself. Discover the dreams and goals that really register on your heart, whether you are twenty, forty, sixty or eighty.

May your life be blessed.

Christine Lauren

From A to Z, I Shall Praise Thee

I trust that this book has been a blessing to you. We have a God worthy of all our love and adoration, worthy of our praise from A to Z.

Almighty One, anchor of my soul.

Bright and Morning Star, Bread of Life, precious bridegroom.

Compassionate Creator, my

Defense and Deliverer, my secure Dwelling place

Eternal, everlasting

Father, faithful and true, I love you!

Giver of every good and perfect gift, my

Hope, my hiding place.

Infinite love, beyond searching out, you are the

Judge, in love with me.

King of Glory, forever dawning

Light, Lord of Hosts, sweet Lamb of God.

Magnificent Maker of heaven and earth, Mighty God!

*N*ame above all names, who neither slumbers nor
sleeps. Nestling me in your arms of love.

*O*verseer of all that is, overshadowing me with
grace and mercy.

*P*rince of Peace, powerful bringer of

*Q*uiet and rest to my soul.

*R*ock under my feet, refuge and

*S*trength, the very strength of my heart.

Shepherd of Israel, my salvation.

*T*ruth you place in my inward parts, your

*U*nderstanding illuminates my being.

*V*igilant, enduring until victory is won in the
deepest recesses of my soul.
Oh, Lord, you are the

*W*ay, wonderful beyond

e*X*pression! My

*Y*outh you renew like the eagle's. Out of

*Z*ion, the perfection of beauty, God has shined!

Christine Lauren

References

1. Psalm 127:3
2. Matthew 7:24-27
3. Genesis 2:7
4. I Thessalonians 5:23
5. Revelation 12:3-9
6. John 10:10
7. John 8:44
8. Ezekiel 36:25-28
9. John 3:16
10. Colossians 1:13
11. Psalm 103:12
12. Micah 7:19
13. Isaiah 1:18
14. II Timothy 3:16
15. Hebrews 4:12
16. Jeremiah 31:33
17. Luke 1:37
18. Matthew 18:20
19. Hebrews 13:8
20. Romans 12:1
21. John 10:14
22. John 10:15
23. John 8:36
24. Luke 4:18
25. Ephesians 3:20
26. Isaiah 55:8
27. Psalm 103:12
28. II Corinthians 5:17
29. John 3:7
30. Psalm 40:5
31. Matthew 4:24
32. Matthew 11:5
33. John 14:12
34. John 1:26-27
35. John 1:29-31
36. John 1:32-34
37. Luke 3:16
38. Matthew 28:18
39. Mark 16:15-18
40. Genesis 1:26-27
41. Genesis 2:18
42. Genesis 2
43. Mark 11:26
44. Deuteronomy 5:29
45. Psalm 61:3-4
46. James 1:17
47. I Thessalonians 4:3-5 & 7
48. II Timothy 2:22
49. I John 3:2-3
50. I Corinthians 6:19
51. Galatians 3:28
52. Revelation 21:23
53. Ephesians 5:27
54. Revelation 21:8
55. Revelation 21:11
56. II Corinthians 11:2
57. Revelation 1:6
58. II Timothy 2:12
59. Ephesians 5:30
60. Ephesians 5:31
61. I Corinthians 6:18
62. I Corinthians 6:19-20
63. II Corinthians 11:14
64. Genesis 2:24
65. Matthew 18:18-20
66. I Corinthians 6:19-20
67. John 15:13
68. Exodus 34:14
69. Matthew 16:4
70. Romans 14:23b
71. II Corinthians 11:14
72. Matthew 7:17
73. I John 1:9
74. Hebrews 8:12
75. Psalm 103:12
76. Ephesians 1:5-6
77. Hebrews 4:12
78. Jeremiah 15:16

79. *John 8:32*
80. *I John 1:9*
81. *Isaiah 61:1*
82. *Psalm 51:10*
83. *Mark 16:17*
84. *Ephesians 4:3*
85. *I John 1:7*
86. *Mark 16:17*
87. *Acts 2:38*
88. *Mathew 3:11*
89. *John 14:26*
90. *Ephesians 1:17*
91. *I Corinthians 12:4-11*
92. *Hebrews 10:25*
93. *3 John 1:3*
94. *Genesis 2:18*
95. *Proverbs 3:5-6*
96. *Mark 11:24*
97. *Matthew 6:13*
98. *Psalm 32:7*
99. *Ephesians 3:17-19*
100. *Ephesians 2:10*
101. *II Timothy 1:7*
102. *Mark 16:17*
103. *II Corinthians 5:17*
104. *Ephesians 1:3*
105. *Psalm 36:5*
106. *Hebrews 13:5b*
107. *Revelation 22:12*

To order additional copies, search by title and author's name at www.amazon.com or put www.createspace.com/3498143 in the URL, not the search bar.

Contact author at feetadancing@gmail.com

OTHER BOOKS AVAILABLE BY CHRISTINE LAUREN

Keys of the Kingdom Revealed

Have you ever wondered what the keys of the kingdom are and how to use them? This book will reveal the answers to you!
To order, go to www.createspace.com/6315809

Health Made Simple! How to Build Good Health in Four Simple Steps

Discover the four components that could help you get your health back on track. Based on 50 years of a health nut's personal experience.
To order, go to www.createspace.com/6112786

Seven Steps Out of Depression

Simply presented, yet effective in bringing hope through specific action steps. Bible based.
To order go to www.createspace.com/3644723

The ABCs of Jesus Coloring Book

An evangelism tool with scripture for each letter of the alphabet, teaching children who Jesus is plus a certificate to frame to celebrate the day of their salvation. Also includes a letter from Jesus welcoming them into His family.
Available in four languages~
For English go to www.createspace.com/3514547
For French go to www.createspace.com/3577656
For German go to www.createspace.com/3633212
For Spanish go to www.createspace.com/3590244

The ABCs of Me Coloring Book

A wonderful evangelism tool with scripture for each letter of the alphabet that will teach children who they are in Christ. Also includes a certificate to frame to celebrate the day of their salvation and a letter of Jesus welcoming them into His family.
To order go to www.createspace.com/3643816

ABCs of Jesus

This book contains the same scripture as found in <u>The ABCs of Jesus Coloring Book</u> with each letter having a response to the scripture on each page of the alphabet. Sized to fit conveniently into a pocket or purse. This book is also an evangelism tool and very fitting as a gift.

To order go to <u>www.createspace.com/7226616</u>

ABCs of Me

This book is a companion book to the ABCs of Jesus companion book because the author strongly believes that when we have an understanding of who Jesus is and who we are in Christ, we have the full spectrum of our identity and the identity of our Lord. Sized to fit conveniently in a pocket or purse. Ideal as a gift or to be used as an evangelism tool. These companion books could be the basis of a great Bible study!

To order go to <u>www.createspace.com/7462521</u>

Stories & Poems of Faith, Wisdom and Kindness

This book is illustrated with color pictures and contains a wide variety of stories and poems for adults and children that will touch their heart and stir the spirit.

To order, go to <u>www.createspace.com/3549099</u>

Wisdom Through Symbols

This book will challenge youth and adults to get their hands on Proverbs in a new way. Reader will work with scriptures as formulas for life expressed in symbols. One of the intents of this book is to show cause and effect regarding the happenings of life so that the reader will not be blindsided by what may come their way in this world.

To order, go to <u>www.createspace.com/3624757</u>

To order, search by title and author's name at www.amazon.com or put www.createspace.com/3498143 in URL, not the search bar.

No minimum purchase required. Books can be shipped in the United States and internationally.

Contact the author at feetadancing@gmail.com